Nicky Epstein's
Fabulous Felted Bags

15 BAGS TO KNIT AND FELT

Editorial Director   *David Codling*
Graphic Design   *Gregory Courtney*
Photography   *Kathryn Martin*
Makeup and Hair Stylist   *Kira Lee*
Clothing Stylist   *Betsy Westman*
Bags Modeled By   *Katie Dunn*

Color Reproduction and Printing   *Regent Publishing Services*

Published and Distributed By   *Unicorn Books and Crafts, Inc.*   <u>*www.unicornbooks.com*</u>

Yarn paks are available for all designs in this book. For purchasing and stockist information, contact *Simply Shetland* at 1-877-743-8526 or visit <u>*www.simplyshetland.net*</u>.

Printed in China

ISBN   1-893063-15-1

3 4 5 6 7 8 9 10

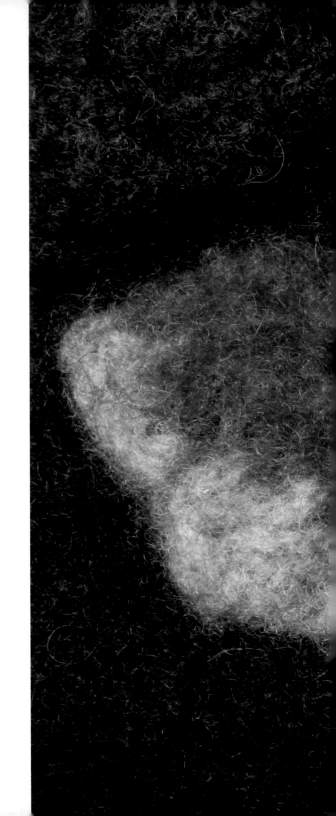

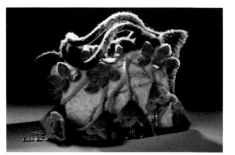

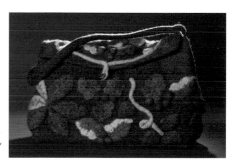

Nicky Epstein's
Fabulous Felted Bags

When asked to do a book of handknit handbags, I jumped at the opportunity, because I love bags—they're practically indispensable! I've incorporated many different shapes and motifs that range from whimsical to haute couture, and have tried to make them functional, fashionable and fun.

You'll find an added element that is very exciting to me . . . they're all . . . *felted*. Felting adds whole new dimensions to the bags—texture . . . durability . . . cohesion . . . and distinctive style. I well know how nerve racking it can be to throw a lovingly-knit project into the uncharted territory of hot and soapy water and hope that the gods of the washing machine will be kind. Not to worry! If you follow my felting hints, it most always works. And the good news—a bag doesn't have to fit! So knit . . . felt . . . and be merry.

Striped Houndstooth

Materials

Jamieson's Shetland Double Knitting—

175 grams MC, Black (999)

50 grams Color A, Sorbet (570)

50 grams Color B, Anemone (616)

50 grams Color C, Chartreuse (365)

50 grams Color D, Lunar (680)

12 large safety pins

1 large snap

Four ¾" gold purse screw-on handle loops (from
   Bag Boutique—www.bagboutique.com) OR
   #HLG screw-on handle loops (from Sunbelt—
   www.sunbeltfasteners.com)

Tapestry needle

Needles

24" circular US 9 (5.5 mm), *or size needed to obtain gauge*

Set of double-pointed US 6 (4 mm)

Size

Approx. 15" wide x 13" high *before felting*

Approx. 11" wide x 12" high *after felting*

Gauge

18 sts/24 rows = 4" in stockinette stitch on US 9

Striped Houndstooth

Stripe Sequence for Front and Back of Bag
With Black (999) as D (dark) color throughout, * work 3 repeats of
Houndstooth Pattern with Color A as L (light), 3 repeats with Color B as L, 3
repeats with Color C as L, and 3 repeats with Color D as L, repeat from *.

Houndstooth Pattern—Multiple of 4 sts
Row 1 (RS) Knit D1, * L1, D3, repeat from * to last 3 sts, end L1, D2.
Row 2 Purl * L3, D1, repeat from *.
Row 3 Knit * L3, D1, repeat from *.
Row 4 Purl D1, * L1, D3, repeat from * to last 3 sts, end L1, D2.

Repeat Rows 1-4.

Front & Back—Make 2
With US 9 and MC, cast on 60 sts.

Row 1 (RS) Knit.
Row 2 Purl.

Work **Houndstooth Pattern** in **Stripe Sequence, AND AT SAME TIME**, cast
on 2 sts at beginning of every row 4 times—68 sts. Continue in pattern until 19
repeats of **Houndstooth Pattern** are complete, ending with RS facing for next
row.

Shape Top
Next Row (RS) Continuing in **Houndstooth Pattern**, work 19 sts, bind off next
30 sts, work 19 sts.

Turn and work each side separately (continuing in **Houndstooth Pattern** as
set), **AND AT SAME TIME**, decrease 1 st at beginning and end of every RS
row until 13 sts remain. Work 1 more row (WS), completing **Houndstooth
Pattern**.

Next Row (RS) Change to MC and knit, decreasing 1 st at beginning and end of
row—11 sts.
Next Row (WS) With MC, purl.

Place sts on holders.

Bag Sides and Bottom—Worked in One Piece
With US 9 and 2 strands of MC held together throughout, cast on 15 sts.
Work in stockinette stitch until piece fits comfortably around edges and
bottom of front (or back) from one handle to the other. Bind off. Sew to front
and back along sides and bottom.

Top Hem—Both Front & Back of Bag
With MC, RS facing, pick up 52 sts along top edge of front, between sts on
holders.

Next Row (WS) Purl.
Next Row (Turning Row) Purl.

Work in stockinette stitch (beginning with a WS row) for 1". Bind off. Fold to
inside of bag and sew down. Repeat for back of bag.

Pocket
With Color D, cast on 21 sts and work in stockinette stitch for 6". Bind off.
Sew to inside back of bag 3" from top.

Strap Handle Holders
Place 11 sts from holder onto US 9.

Next Row (RS) K1, (k2tog) 5 times—6 sts.

Work in stockinette stitch for 3". Bind off. Fold in half and sew down. Repeat
for opposite side.

Felt Bag

See *Felting Instructions* on page 80. Screw metal strap handles onto strap handle holders.

Roses—Make 3 each in Colors A, B, C & D (12 Total)

With US 9, cast on 101 sts. Work as follows:

Row 1 (WS) Purl.
Row 2 K2, * k1 and slip it back to left-hand needle; with right-handle needle, lift next 8 sts, 1 st at a time, over this st and off needle, yo twice, k the first st again, k2, repeat from * to end.
Row 3 P1, * p2tog, drop first yo of previous row, k into the front, back, front, back and front again in second yo (5 sts made), p1, repeat from *, end p1.
Row 4 Knit.

Bind off in knit. Roll bound-off edge to form petals and stitch in place.

Corkscrews—Make 3 each in Colors A, B, C & D (12 Total)

With US 9, cast on 20 sts *very loosely* (use two needles, if necessary).

Row 1 (RS) Knit into front, back, and front again of each st (3 sts made in each st)—60 sts on needle.
Row 2 Bind off purlwise.

Twist each into a corkscrew shape. Run large safety pin through each corkscrew to hold its shape during felting process.

Straps

With US 6 double-pointed needles and MC, cast on 4 sts. Work knit cord as follows: * k4, without turning, slide sts to opposite end of needle, repeat from * until cord measures approx. 116" long. Bind off.

Felt Roses, Corkscrews & Strap

See *Felting Instructions* on page 80. Check corkscrews often during felting process, as they may become tangled or stretched. After felting, roses and corkscrews may need reshaping.

Attach Straps, Roses & Corkscrews

Cut felted cord in half. Insert cord into metal handle loops on each side of bag and sew ends together. Sew 3 roses and 3 corkscrews to upper corners of front and back of bag.

Attach Snap

Sew snap to center top, on front and back.

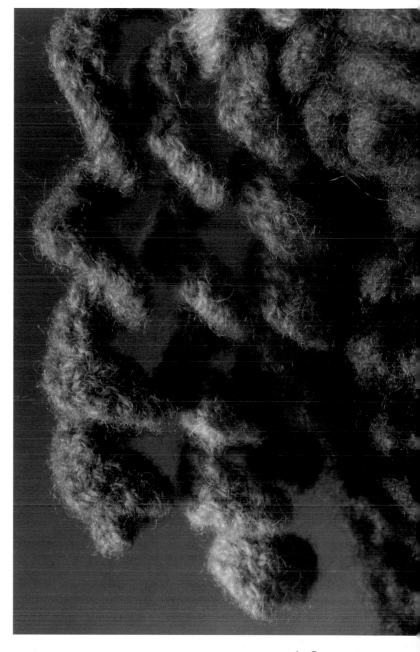

Bobbles &
Brambles

Materials
Jamieson's Shetland Heather Aran—
150 grams Color A, Mirrydancers (1400)
200 grams Color B, Lacquer (1220)

Two 8½" black acrylic ring handles
  (#27214 from Sunbelt—www.sunbeltfastener.com)
Tapestry needle

Needles
US 11 (8 mm), *or size needed to obtain gauge*

Size
Approx. 16" wide x 18" high *before felting*
Approx. 18" wide x 16" inches high *after felting*

Gauge
15 sts/18 rows = 4" in pattern on US 11

Bobbles & Brambles

Note

Due to nature of stitch pattern, bag becomes wider and shorter when felted.

Stitch Pattern

Multiple of 5 sts plus 1—Colors A and B

Row 1 (WS) With Color A, purl.
Row 2 With Color A, knit.
Row 3 With Color A, p1, * p1, wrapping yarn around needle twice, p2, p1, wrapping yarn around twice, p1, repeat from * to end.
Row 4 With Color B, k1, * slip 1 wyib, dropping extra wrap, k2, slip 1 wyib, dropping extra wrap, (k1, yo, k1, yo, k1) in next st. Repeat from * to last 5 sts, end slip 1 wyib, dropping extra wrap, k2, slip 1 wyib, dropping extra wrap, k1.
Row 5 With Color B, p1, * slip 1 wyif, p2, slip 1 wyif, k5, repeat from * end slip 1 wyif, p2, slip 1, p1.
Row 6 With Color B, k1, * slip 1 wyib, k2, slip 1 wyib, p5, repeat from *, end slip 1 wyib, k2, slip 1 wyib, k1.
Row 7 With Color B, p1 * slip 1 wyif, p2, slip 1 wyif, k2tog, k3tog, pass the k2tog st over the k3tog st, repeat from *, end slip 1 wyif, p2, slip 1 wyif, p1.
Row 8 With Color A, k1, * drop elongated st wyib off needle to front of work, slip next 2 sts wyib to right-hand needle, drop next elongated st wyib off needle. With left-hand needle, pick up first elongated st, slip the 2 sts back to left-hand needle, then pick up second elongated st onto left-hand needle, k5, repeat from *.

Repeat Rows 1-8.

Purse Sides—Make 2

Starting at purse bottom, with Color B, cast on 61 sts. Work the 8 rows of **Stitch Pattern** until piece measures approx. 18", ending after working Row 8 of **Stitch Pattern** (WS facing for next row).

Make Hem

With Color B, purl, knit 2 rows (turning ridge). Work in stockinette stitch for 2". Bind off.

Pocket

With Color A, cast on 31 sts. Work in stockinette stitch for 8½". Bind off. Sew to center of back 2½" below top.

Bow

With Color B, cast on 17 sts. Work in stockinette stitch for 14½". Bind off. With RS together, sew cast-on edge to bound-off edge. Thread Color B onto tapestry needle, pinch bow with seam at center and sew to form bow.

Center Band of Bow

With Color B, cast on 5 sts. Work in stockinette stitch for 2". Wrap around center of bow and sew. Agitate bow in warm water. When dry, sew to center top of bag 1" down.

Felting & Finishing

Sew side and bottom seams. Felt bag, following *Felting Instructions* on page 80. After felting is complete and bag is dry, fold hems over handles and sew in place.

Tropicana

Materials
Jamieson's Shetland Double Knitting—
300 grams MC, Black (999)

25 grams Crimson (525)	25 grams Cornfield (410)
25 grams Teviot (136)	25 grams Cobalt (684)
25 grams Mooskit (106)	25 grams Aubretia (1300)
25 grams Anemone (616)	25 grams Lagoon (660)
25 grams Mint (770)	25 grams Amber (478)
25 grams Chartreuse (365)	25 grams Leprechaun (259)
25 grams Moss (147)	25 grams Coffee (880)
25 grams Burnt Umber (1190)	

Two ½" dowels—approx. 20½" long
4 large safety pins
Large black snap
Tapestry needle

Needles
US 9 (5.5 mm), *or size needed to obtain gauge*
Set of double-pointed US 6 (4 mm)

Size
Approx. 27" wide x 31" high *before felting*
Approx. 20" wide x 24" high *after felting*

Gauge
17 sts/23 rows = 4" in stockinette stitch on US 9

Note

Work parrot motif in intarsia method or work in duplicate stitch after background is complete (motif on bag shown in photo is worked in duplicate stitch).

Front

With US 9 and MC, cast on 115 sts. Work in stockinette stitch for 18 rows, ending with RS facing for next row. Work 133 rows of **Front Chart**. When chart is complete, continue in stockinette stitch with MC, decreasing 1 st at beginning and end of next 10 RS rows as follows: k1, ssk, knit to last 3 sts, k2tog, k1—95 sts.

Make Turning Ridge

Next Row (RS) Purl.
Next Row (WS) Purl.

Continue in stockinette stitch for 10 rows for hem, increasing 1 st at beginning and end of every RS row 3 times—101 sts. Purl 1 row. Bind off.

Back

Work same as for front following **Back Chart**.

Pocket

With US 9 and MC, cast on 42 sts. Work in stockinette stitch until pocket measures 9". Bind off.

Work Embroidery, Attach Pocket and Sew Seams

Embroider leaf veins, berries and parrot feathers where shown in charts. Sew pocket to inside center of back. Sew bottom. Sew side seams up to where shaping begins. Fold hem and sew to inside, leaving sides open to insert dowels. Felt bag, following **Felting Instructions** on page 80.

Handles—Make 2

With MC and US 6 double-pointed needles, cast on 4 sts. Work knit cord as follows: * k4, without turning, slide sts to opposite end of needle, repeat from * until cord measures 138". Bind off. Fold each cord 4 times and pin together with safety pins to keep from tangling in washing machine. Felt the cord, following **Felting Instructions** on page 80. When cord is felted, fold each cord in half and make twisted cord approximately 23" long. Sew one handle each to front and back centered 10" apart. Run dowel through hem on both front and back and stitch open ends closed. Sew snap to inside center.

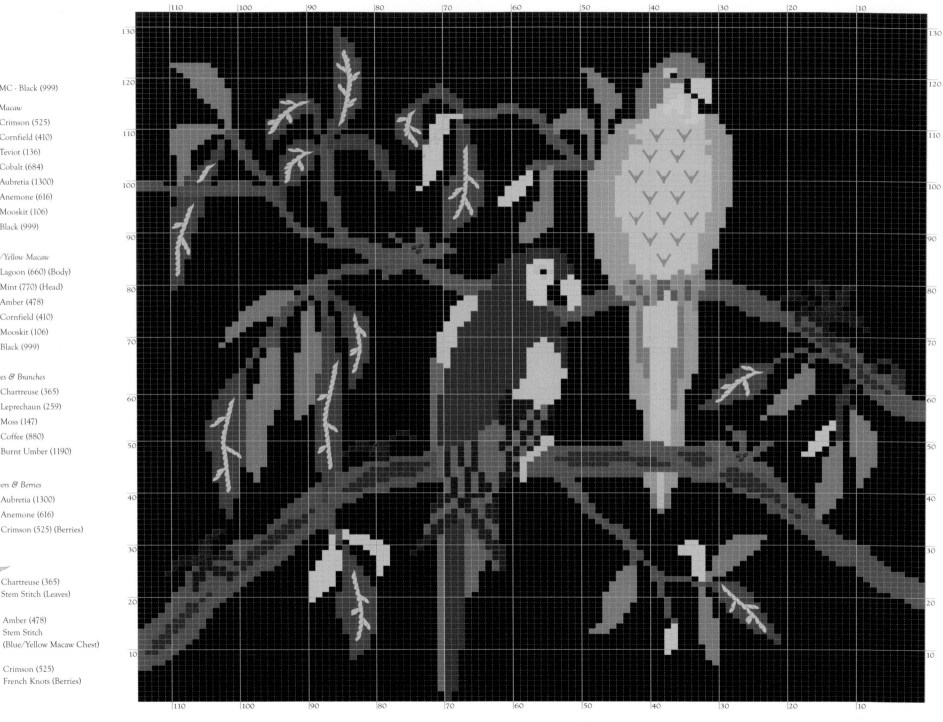

MC - Black (999)

Red Macaw
Crimson (525)
Cornfield (410)
Teviot (136)
Cobalt (684)
Aubretia (1300)
Anemone (616)
Mooskit (106)
Black (999)

Blue/Yellow Macaw
Lagoon (660) (Body)
Mint (770) (Head)
Amber (478)
Cornfield (410)
Mooskit (106)
Black (999)

Leaves & Branches
Chartreuse (365)
Leprechaun (259)
Moss (147)
Coffee (880)
Burnt Umber (1190)

Flowers & Berries
Aubretia (1300)
Anemone (616)
Crimson (525) (Berries)

Chartreuse (365)
Stem Stitch (Leaves)

Amber (478)
Stem Stitch
(Blue/Yellow Macaw Chest)

Crimson (525)
French Knots (Berries)

Tropicana - Front Chart

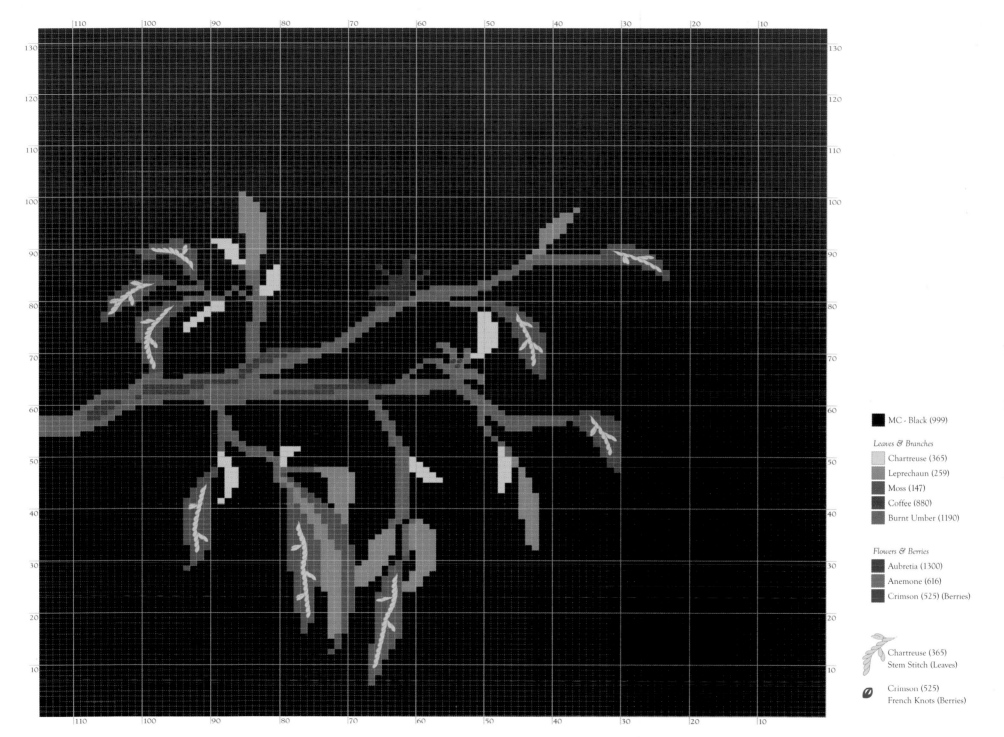

Tropicana - Back Chart

MC - Black (999)

Leaves & Branches

Chartreuse (365)

Leprechaun (259)

Moss (147)

Coffee (880)

Burnt Umber (1190)

Flowers & Berries

Aubretia (1300)

Anemone (616)

Crimson (525) (Berries)

Chartreuse (365)
Stem Stitch (Leaves)

Crimson (525)
French Knots (Berries)

Circles

Materials
Jamieson's Shetland Double Knitting—
150 grams Color A, Slate (125)
50 grams Color B, Old Rose (556)
50 grams Color C, Black (999)

4 large safety pins
Tapestry needle

Needles
24" circular US 9 (5.5 mm), *or size needed to obtain gauge*
Set of double-pointed US 6 (4 mm)

Size
Approx. 28½" wide x 20½" high *before felting*
Approx. 11½" wide x 13" high *after felting*

Gauge
17 sts/23 rows = 4" in stockinette stitch on US 9

Bag

With US 9 and Color A, cast on 122 sts.

* With Color A, beginning with RS, work in stockinette stitch for 18 rows, ending with RS facing for next row. Change to Color C, knit 1 row, purl 1 row, repeat from * 4 times more. With Color A, continue in stockinette stitch for 18 rows.

Hem

Next Row (RS) (Turning Row) Purl.

With WS facing for next row, continue in stockinette stitch for 2". Bind off.

Bottom

With US 9 and double strand of Color A, RS facing, pick up 122 sts around bottom edge. With tapestry needle, run contrasting waste thread through these sts for bottom edge cord to be knitted later.

Next Row (WS) Purl.

Work bottom of bag as follows:

Row 1 (RS) K1, (k2tog, k10) 10 times, k1—112 sts.
Rows 2, 4, 6, 8, 10, 12, 14, 16, 18, 20 & 22 Purl.
Row 3 K1, (k2tog, k9) 10 times, k1—102 sts.
Row 5 K1, (k2tog, k8) 10 times, k1—92 sts.
Row 7 K1, (k2tog, k7) 10 times, k1—82 sts.
Row 9 Purl.
Row 11 K1, (k2tog, k6) 10 times, k1—72 sts.
Row 13 K1, (k2tog, k5) 10 times, k1—62 sts.

Row 15 K1, (k2tog, k4) 10 times, k1—52 sts.
Row 17 K1, (k2tog, k3) 10 times, k1—42 sts.
Row 19 K1, (k2tog, k2) 10 times, k1—32 sts.
Row 21 K1, (k2tog, k1) 10 times, k1—22 sts.
Row 23 K1, (k2tog) 10 times, k1—12 sts.
Row 24 (P2tog) 6 times—6 sts.

Cut yarn leaving long end. With tapestry needle, thread end through remaining sts. Pull tight to close hole and fasten securely.

Bottom Edge Cord

With Color C, RS facing, pick up 122 sts from waste yarn (removing waste yarn as you go) and beginning with purl row, work in stockinette stitch for 1¼". Bind off. Fold in half and sew to form cord around bottom edge of bag.

Circles—Make 42

With Color B and US 6 double-pointed needles, cast on 6 sts. Work knit cord as follows: * k6, without turning, slide sts to opposite end of needle, repeat from * for 35 rows. Bind off. Sew cast-on edge to bound-off edge to form circle.

Attach Circles to Bag

Thread double strand of black (Color C) onto tapestry needle and sew circles to bag every 15th st (excluding selvedge sts) along thin horizontal lines as follows: run tapestry needle through seam of circle and sew to bag by wrapping yarn around the circle and through the bag on black line 4 times, hiding the seam. ***There will be 7 circles along each of the 5 thin horizontal lines (35 circles in all—5 circles are*** left over to attach to side seam after it is sewn; 2 circles are left over to attach to handle).

Sew bag seam from center bottom to top hem. Sew remaining 5 circles along seam at horizontal black lines in same manner as above.

Drawstring

With US 6 double-pointed needles and Color C, cast on 6 sts and work cord as follows: * k6, without turning, slide sts to opposite end of needle, repeat from * until cord measures 73". Bind off. Sew a circle to each end of cording in manner described above.

Felting & Finishing

Felt bag, following ***Felting Instructions*** on page 80. When felting, fold cord and secure with large safety pins to keep it from knotting during felting process—check often while washing to be sure it doesn't tangle. After bag is felted and dry, fold hem at turning row and sew to inside, leaving ½" space for cord. Insert large safety pin into one end of cord and run cord through hem. *Cord makes drawstring to open and close bag.*

Flapper

Materials

Jamieson's Shetland Double Knitting—
125 grams Color A, Mint (770)
25 grams Color B, Granny Smith (1140)
50 grams Color C, Chartreuse (365)
25 grams Color D, Ivy (815)
25 grams Color E, Apple (785)

Decorative pin (#RF25 from Sunbelt,
 www.sunbeltfasteners.com)
Large snap

Needles

3 straight US 9 (5.5 mm), *or size needed to obtain gauge*
Set of double-pointed US 9 (5.5 mm)

Size

Approx. 13" wide x 13" high *before felting*
Approx. 10" wide x 9" high *after felting*

Gauge

17 sts/23 rows = 4" in stockinette stitch on US 9

Flapper

Seed Stitch
Row 1 (RS) * K1, p1, repeat from *.
Row 2 Knit the purl sts and purl the knit sts as they face you.

Repeat Rows 1-2.

Flap Color Sequence for Front of Bag—From Left
1st Row (Bottom Row) D D A A B B
2nd Row E A A A C C
3rd Row B B C C D D
4th Row D D A A C C
5th Row E E B B B A
6th Row (Top Row) C C D D E E

Flap Color Sequence for Back of Bag—From Left
1st Row (Bottom Row) D D C C A A
2nd Row E E B B B E
3rd Row B A A A C C
4th Row C C D D E E
5th Row E E E B B A
6th Row (Top Row) B B C C D D

Front

With US 9 and Color A (Mint—background color), cast on 56 sts (first and last sts are selvedge stitches). *With Color A, work in stockinette stitch for 12 rows. Leave sts on needle and set aside. Following **Flap Color Sequence for Front of Bag**, with another US 9 and first color in the sequence, cast on 9 sts. Work in **Seed Stitch** for 18 rows. Break yarn and leave sts on needle—push flap to capped end of needle—one flap made. On same needle, cast on 9 sts and work flap in next color in the sequence. Continue in this way until there are 6 flaps on needle—one row of flaps complete. With RS facing, holding needle with flaps in front of needle with background color, knit first st (selvedge st), then knit each flap st together with each background st, then knit the last st

(selvedge st). With Color A, purl next row. Repeat from * until the 6 rows of flaps are complete. Continuing in Color A, make hem as follows:

Make Hem
Next Row (WS) Purl.
Next Row Purl.

Continue in stockinette stitch and Color A until hem measures 1". Bind off.

Back
Work same as for front of bag, following **Flap Color Sequence for Back of Bag**.

Pocket
With US 9 and Color B (or color of your choice), cast on 29 sts. Work in stockinette stitch until pocket measures 7". Bind off.

Finishing & Felting
Weave in ends. Sew pocket to inside center of front of bag approx. 4" down from top. Sew side and bottom seams. Fold hem down and sew to inside.

Handle—Make Eight 8" Cords, Two 3" Cords and One 14" Cord
With Color C and US 9 double-pointed needles, cast on 5 sts. Work knit cord as follows: * k5, without turning, slide sts to opposite end of needle, repeat from * until cord measures correct length. [Sew ends of one 8" cord together to form circle, * loop next 8" cord through circle and sew to create a chain. Repeat from * two times more.] Repeat from [to] to create second part of handle. For center part of handle, sew ends of 14" cord together. Loop side cord chains through connecting cord on each side. Loop one of the 3" cords through bottom circle of a chain link and with a tapestry needle pull bound-off and cast-on threads through to inside of bag at side seam and knot. Repeat with other end of handle. Felt bag, following ***Felting Instructions*** on page 80. Check often to be sure handle doesn't tangle during washing. Sew snap to inside of bag at top centers. Attach decorative pin, if used.

S'wanderful

Materials
Jamieson's Shetland Heather Aran—
300 grams MC, Ivory (343)
50 grams Color A, Mirrydancers (1400)
50 grams Color B, Gingersnap (331)

16" of feathers
Small amount of Polyfil™ for head
Quilt batting for neck
Two ½" black round buttons for eyes
Large snap
Stitch holders
Tapestry needle

Needles
US 11 (8 mm), *or size needed to obtain gauge*

Size
Approx. 19" wide x 19" high; approx. 48"
  from neck to tip of beak *before felting*
Approx. 16" wide x 12" high; approx. 44"
  from neck to tip of beak *after felting*

Gauge
17 sts/24 rows = 4" in stockinette stitch on US 11

S'wanderful

Front
With US 11 and MC, cast on 71 sts. Work in stockinette stitch, **AND AT SAME TIME**, cast on 2 sts at beginning of next 6 rows—83 sts. Continue without further shaping until piece measures 19" from cast-on edge.

Next Row (RS) K58 sts, place remaining 25 sts on holder.

Make Hem
Next Row (WS) Knit.

Continue in stockinette stitch for 2". Bind off.

Back
Work same as for front until piece measures 19" from cast-on edge.

Next Row (RS) K25 sts and place on holder, knit remaining 58 sts.

Make Hem
Next Row (WS) Knit.

Continue in stockinette stitch for 2". Bind off.

Join Front & Back
Sew bottom and side seams.

Neck
Place 25 sts from each holder onto needle—50 sts.

Next Row (RS) Knit, decreasing 15 sts evenly spaced across row—35 sts.

Work remaining 35 sts in stockinette stitch for 2", ending with RS facing for next row.

Next Row (RS) K2tog, k31, k2tog—33 sts.

Continue in stockinette stitch until neck measures 31", ending with RS facing for next row.

Head
Next Row (RS) Knit into front and back of every st—66 sts.
Next Row P33, m1, p33—67 sts.

Continue in stockinette stitch for 3½", ending with WS facing for next row.

Work **Head & Neck Chart** in stockinette stitch, beginning with WS row, working decreases on RS rows at edges as shown and double decreases (*slip 2 sts together knitwise, k1, pass the 2 slipped sts over the knit st*) on center 3 sts (indicated by an "X" on chart)—41 sts remain when chart is complete.

Next Row (RS) With Color C, decrease 6 sts evenly spaced across row—35 sts remain.

Continue with Color C, working double decreases on center 3 sts on every 4th RS row and decrease 1 st at beginning and end of every 4th row until 11 sts remain, ending with WS facing for next row. Change to Color B and continue decreases until 4

sts remain. Pass 2nd, 3rd, 4th, stitch over 1st stitch. Tie off.

Finishing
Sew head seams, stuff head lightly with Polyfil™. Cut batting doubled 32" x 8". Roll long side to form a 5" tube and sew closed with sewing thread. Lay tube onto WS of neck and sew neck together from RS. Secure batting to top and bottom of neck with sewing thread. With Color B, work a line with stem stitch on both sides of beak (see photo). Fold and sew together top of beak following marked red line on chart.

Neck Plug
With Color A, cast on 6 sts. Work in stockinette stitch, increasing 1 st at beginning and end of every RS row until there are 12 sts on needle. Continue in stockinette stitch for 3", decreasing 1 st at beginning and end of every other row until 6 sts remain. Bind off. Sew plug into bottom of neck.

Pocket
With MC, cast on 31 sts. Work in stockinette stitch until pocket measures 6½". Bind off. Sew to center inside back. Sew snap to inside of bag at top centers. Felt bag, following **Felting Instructions** on page 80. Check often during felting process to make sure neck doesn't twist. Sew button eyes in place (see chart). Sew feathers to top right side of purse opening. Bend neck and sew head to opposite side of purse, 3" from top.

S'wanderful

S'wanderful - Head & Beak Chart

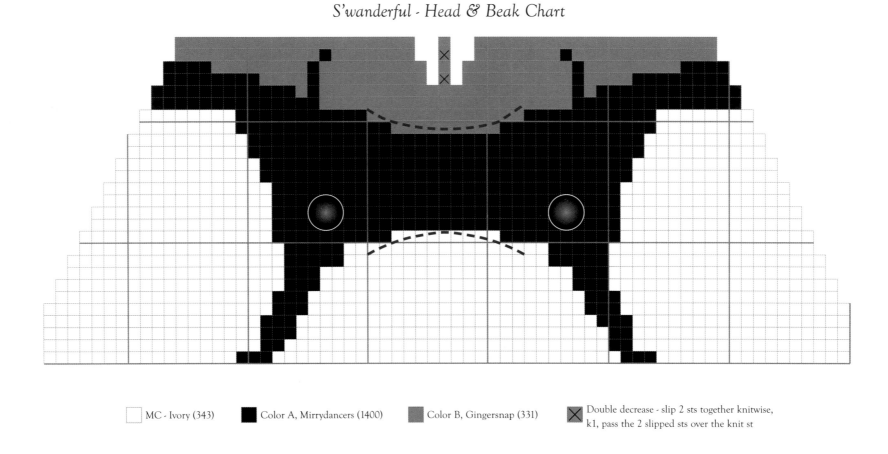

| | MC - Ivory (343) | ■ Color A, Mirrydancers (1400) | ■ Color B, Gingersnap (331) | ☒ Double decrease - slip 2 sts together knitwise, k1, pass the 2 slipped sts over the knit st |

Fuschias

Materials
Jamieson's Shetland Double Knitting—
150 grams Color A, Atlantic (150)
50 grams Color B, Rye (140)
25 grams Color C, Willow (769)
50 grams Color D, Eucalyptus (794)
25 grams Color E, Rose (550)
25 grams Color F, Sorbet (570)
25 grams Color G, Cherry (580)

Bead fringe
5 large safety pins
Large snap

Needles
US 10 (6 mm), *or size needed to obtain gauge*
Set of 2 double-pointed US 8 (5 mm)

Size
Approx. 18" wide x 19" high *before felting*
Approx. 15" wide x 11" high *after felting*

Gauge
18 sts/22 rows = 4" in stockinette stitch on US 10

Fuschias

Note
Work background stems in duplicate st. Applique leaves and stem cords onto bag.

Front
With US 10 and Color A, cast on 80 sts. Work in stockinette stitch for 15 rows, ending with RS facing for next row. Work the 72 rows of **Chart**.

Continuing with Color A only, work in stockinette stitch for 15 rows.

Make Hem
Next Row (RS) Purl.
Next Row Purl.

Continue in stockinette stitch for 1¾". Bind off.

Back
With US 10 and Color A, cast on 80 sts. Work in stockinette stitch for 102 rows. Make hem same as for front. Fold hem and sew to inside.

Flowers—Make 5
With US 10 and Color E, cast on 57 sts.

Row 1 RS Purl.
Row 2 K2, * k1, slip this st back to left-hand needle, lift the next 8 sts on left-hand needle over this st and off needle, [yo] twice, knit the first st again, k2, repeat from * to end.
Row 3 P1, * p2tog, drop 1 yo, [knit into front and back of next st (remaining yo)] twice, p1, repeat from *, end last repeat p2—32 sts.
Rows 4, 6 & 8 With Color F, * p2, k1, repeat from *, end p2.
Rows 5 & 7 * K2, p1, repeat from *, end k2.
Row 9 With Color G, * k2tog, p2tog, repeat from *—16 sts.
Rows 10–11 * K1, p1, repeat from *.
Row 12 * K2tog, repeat from *—8 sts.

Row 13 * P2tog, repeat form *—4 sts.

Change to US 8 double-pointed needles and work stem cords as follows:

Attached Cord Stems
With Color C, k2, k2tog—3 sts. * Without turning, slide sts to opposite end of needle, k3, repeat from *. When stem measures 4", bind off. Leave long tail for attaching to bag. Work remaining four flowers, three with 6" cord stems and one with an 8" cord stem. Sew side seams of flowers and weave in ends.

Leaves—Make 24
With US 10 and Color D, cast on 5 sts.

Row 1 (RS) K2, yo, k1, yo, k2—7 sts.
Row 2 (and all WS rows) Purl.
Row 3 K3, yo, k1, yo, k3—9 sts.
Row 5 K4, yo, k1, yo, k4—11 sts.
Row 7 Ssk, k7, k2tog—9 sts.
Row 9 Ssk, k5, k2tog—7 sts.
Row 11 Ssk, k3, k2tog—5 sts.
Row 13 Ssk, k1, k2tog—3 sts.
Row 15 Slip 1, k2tog, psso—1 st. Fasten off.

Stems
With Color D, work stems in duplicate stitch following chart.

Attach Leaves
Sew lower half of leaves to bag, referring to chart for leaf placement. Sew indicated part of cord only to background.

Pocket
With Color A, cast on 31 sts. Work in stockinette stitch for 8". Bind off. Sew to inside of bag at center top below hem.

Handles—Make 2

With US 8 double-pointed needles and 2 strands of Color A held together, cast on 12 sts. Work in stockinette stitch for 4 rows.

Next Row (RS) (Decrease Row) K1, ssk, knit to last 3 sts, k2tog, k1.
Next Row Purl.

Repeat these 2 rows twice more—6 sts remain. Work knit cord as follows: * k6, without turning, slide sts to opposite end of needle, repeat from * until cord measures 18".

Next Row (RS) (Increase Row) K1, knit into front and back of next st, knit to last 2 sts, knit into front and back of next stitch, k1.
Next Row Purl.

Repeat these 2 rows twice more—12 sts on needle. Work 4 rows in stockinette stitch. Bind off.

Finishing & Felting

Sew handles 3" from outer edges onto both front and back of bag. Soak flowers and agitate by hand. Sew ends of stem cords to bag where shown on **Chart** (unattached part of stem cord will dangle—see photographs). Pin each flower to bag so cords don't get tangled during felting. Felt bag, following **Felting Instructions** on page 80. Sew 3 bead fringe lengths to each flower center. Sew snap to inside of bag at top centers.

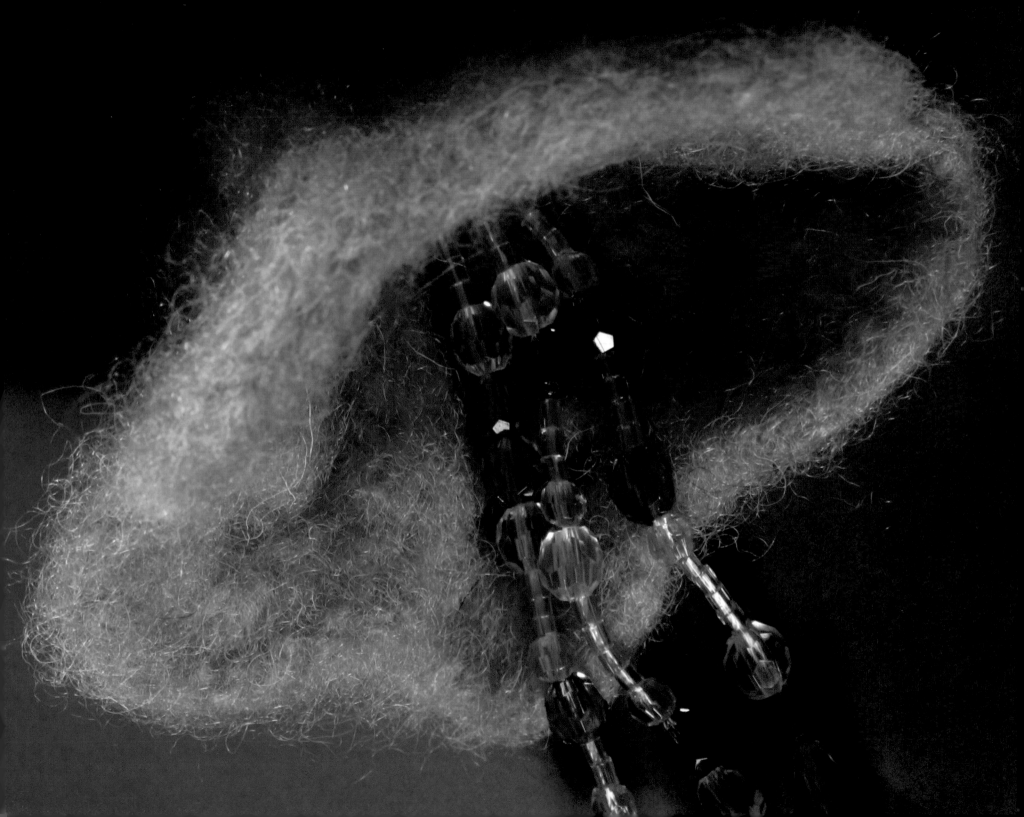

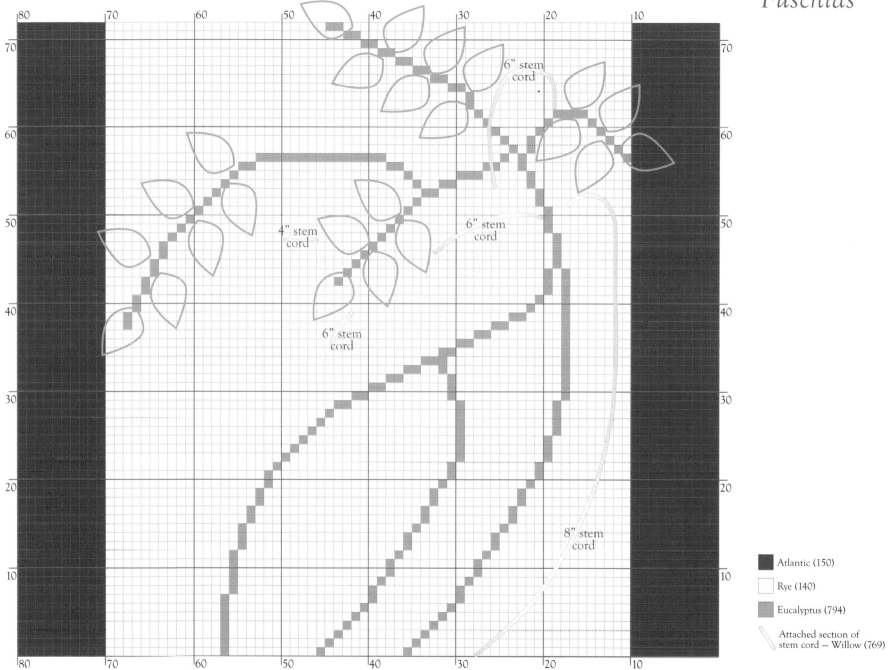

6" stem cord

4" stem cord

6" stem cord

6" stem cord

8" stem cord

■ Atlantic (150)

□ Rye (140)

■ Eucalyptus (794)

Attached section of
stem cord — Willow (769)

Cat & Mouse

Materials
Jamieson's Shetland Heather Aran—
200 grams Color A, Charcoal (126)
50 grams Color B, Ivory (343)
Jamieson's Shetland Double Knitting—
25 grams Color C, Sorbet (570)
Jamieson's 2-Ply Shetland Spindrift—
25 grams Color D, Natural White (104)
  (optional for mouse)

Snap
Quilt batting for cat tail
Polyfil™ for cat head and mouse
Two 18 mm cat eyes
  (Bel-Tree Corporation, Strongville, Ohio 44136)
6 cat whiskers (clear or white plastic)
Small amount of black embroidery floss
Tapestry needle

Needles
For Cat US 11 (8 mm), *or size needed to obtain gauge*
For Mouse Set of double-pointed US 2 (3 mm)

Size
Approx. 18" in diameter *before felting*
Approx. 12" in diameter *after felting*

Gauge
13 sts/16 rows = 4" in stockinette stitch on US 11

Cat & Mouse

CAT

Back

With Color A, cast on 160 sts. Knit one row. Purl one row. Continue as follows:

Row 1 (RS) * K2tog, k14, repeat from *—150 sts.
Row 2 (and all WS rows) Purl.
Row 3 * K2tog, k13, repeat from *—140 sts.
Row 5 * K2tog, k12, repeat from *—130 sts.
Row 7 * K2tog, k11, repeat from *—120 sts.
Row 9 * K2tog, k10, repeat from *—110 sts.
Row 11 * K2tog, k9, repeat from *—100 sts.
Row 13 * K2tog, k8, repeat from *—90 sts.
Row 15 * K2tog, k7, repeat from *—80 sts.
Row 17 * K2tog, k6, repeat from *—70 sts.
Row 19 * K2tog, k5, repeat from *—60 sts.
Row 21 * K2tog, k4, repeat from *—50 sts.
Row 23 * K2tog, k3, repeat from *—40 sts.
Row 25 * K2tog, k2, repeat from *—30 sts.
Row 27 * K2tog, k1, repeat from *—20 sts.
Row 29 * K2tog, rep from *—10 sts.
Row 30 Purl.

Break yarn, thread tail onto tapestry needle, run through remaining sts and secure to inside. Sew seam to form circle.

Front

With Color A, cast on 160 sts. Purl 1 row. Knit 1 row.

Next Row (WS) With Color A, p60; with Color B, p40; with Color A, p60.

Work Rows 1-30 same as for back, allowing Color B to decrease in pattern. Break yarn, thread tail onto tapestry needle, run through remaining sts and secure to inside. Sew seam to form circle.

Head

With Color A, cast on 40 sts.

Row 1 (RS) Knit.
Row 2 Purl into front and back of every st—80 sts.

Continue in stockinette stitch for 2", ending with WS facing for next row.

Next Row (WS) With Color A, p35; with Color B, p10; with Color A, p35.

Continue in stockinette stitch, decreasing same as for back beginning with Row 17, allowing Color B to decrease in pattern. Break yarn, leaving a long tail. Thread tail onto tapestry needle, run through remaining sts and secure to inside. Sew seam to form circle.

Ears

With 2 strands of Color A held together throughout, cast on 9 sts. Work in stockinette stitch for 4 rows. Continue in stockinette stitch, **AND AT SAME TIME**, decrease 1 st at beginning and end of every RS row until 3 sts remain, ending with RS facing for next row.

Next Row (RS) Slip 1, k2tog, psso. Run thread through remaining st.

Thread Color B onto tapestry needle and duplicate stitch ear centers (2 rows of 3 sts and 2 rows of 1 st (see photo).

Tail

With Color B, cast on 6 sts. Work in stockinette stitch, **AND AT SAME TIME**, increase 1 st at beginning and end of every other row 6 times—18 sts. Continue in stockinette stitch without further shaping for 10 more rows. Change to Color A and continue in stockinette stitch until piece measures 32" from cast-on edge. Bind off. Cut batting doubled 30" x 4". Roll long side to form 3" tube and sew closed with sewing thread. Place batting roll on WS of tail, tack down and sew tail seam.

Nose

With 2 strands of Color C held together throughout, cast on 5 sts.

Row 1 (RS) Knit.
Row 2 Purl.
Row 3 Ssk, k1, k2tog.
Row 4 Purl.
Row 5 Slip 1, k2tog, psso. Run thread through remaining st.

Finishing & Felting

Sew ears and nose to face. Sew circles together leaving 18" open at top. With Color C, embroider mouth in stem stitch. Felt head, tail, and body following **Felting Instructions** on page 80. *Felted circles may not lay flat. If necessary, make flat by pleating where head and tail are sewn on. When* felting is complete, attach eyes to head, pull whiskers through to RS of face. Stuff head with Polyfil™ and sew to body. Sew snap to inside of bag at top centers. Sew tail to each end of bag opening.

MOUSE
Tail
With double-pointed US 2 and Color D, cast on 3 sts. * K3, without turning, slide sts to opposite end of needle, repeat from * until tail measures 3½".

Next Row (RS) Yo, * k1, cast on 1 st, rep *—7 sts.
Next Row Purl.
Next Row Yo, * k1, cast on 1 st, rep from *—15 sts.
Next Row Purl.
Next Row Knit, increasing 8 sts evenly across row—23 sts.

Continue in stockinette stitch for 2".

Shape Head
Row 1 (RS) K5, *dbl dec**, k7, dbl dec, k5—19 sts.
Row 2 (and all WS rows) Purl.
Row 3 K4, dbl dec, k5, dbl dec, k4—15 sts.
Row 5 K3, dbl dec, k3, dbl dec, k3—11 sts.

Row 7 K2, dbl dec, k1, dbl dec, k2—7 sts.
Row 9 K2, dbl dec, k2—5 sts.

*dbl dec - Slip 2 sts together knitwise, k1, pass the 2 slipped sts over the knit st.

Thread tail on tapestry needle, run through remaining sts, pull tightly and secure. Sew seam, leaving opening. Stuff lightly with Polyfil™ and sew remaining seam.

Ears—Make 2
With US 2 and Color D, cast on 5 sts.

Row 1 (RS) Knit.
Row 2 Purl.
Row 3 K1, *dbl dec*, k1.
Row 4 Purl.
Row 5 dbl dec. Fasten off remaining st.

Sew ears to side of head at first dbl dec. With black embroidery floss, make french knot for eyes and stem stitch for mouth (see photograph). Felt mouse, following *Felting Instructions* on page 80. Sew tail to cat's mouth.

Yei Figures

Materials
Jamieson's Shetland Double Knitting—
250 grams MC, Dark Navy (730)
25 grams Color A, Mooskit (106)
25 grams Color B, Mint (770)
25 grams Color C, Crimson (525)
25 grams Color D, Amber (478)
25 grams Color E, Flax (375)
25 grams Color F, Sapphire (676)

Two 7/16" dowels—approx. 19½" long
Small beads for necklaces on figures
Safety pins
Large snap
Tapestry needle

Needles
US 9 (5.5 mm), *or size needed to obtain gauge*
Set of double-pointed US 8 (5 mm)

Size
Approx. 21" wide x 23" high *before felting*
Approx. 21" wide x 16" high *after felting**
*Duplicate stitch prevents bag from shrinking in width.

Gauge
17 sts/23 rows = 4" in stockinette stitch on US 9

Yei Figures

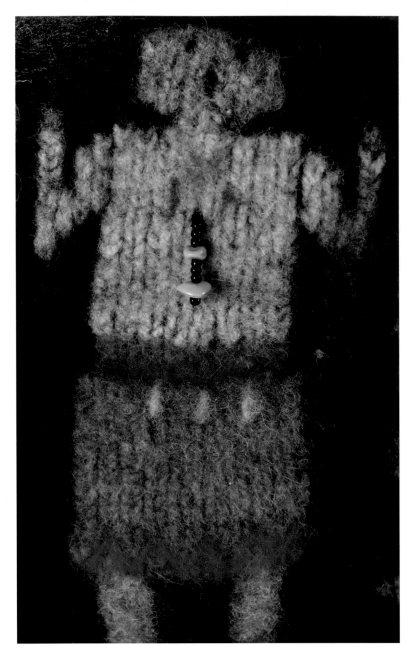

Nicky Epstein's *Fabulous Felted Bags*

Note

Bag shown was knitted according to instructions below. Alternatively, colorwork can be knitted using intarsia method.

Front & Back—Both Alike

With US 9 and MC, cast on 92 sts. Work in stockinette stitch for 122 rows. Continuing in stockinette stitch, work 2 rows in Color A, 2 rows in Color B, 4 rows in Color C, and 2 rows in Color E.

Make Hem

With Color E, purl 3 rows. Change to MC and work in stockinette stitch for 1½". Bind off. Following **Chart**, work borders and figures in duplicate stitch. Work faces, necklaces, skirt decorations and other embellishments in stem stitch. Fold hem and sew to inside, leaving ends open to insert dowels after felting. Sew side seams, leaving 3½" open at top where corded handle is attached after felting.

Felting & Finishing

Felt bag, following *Felting Instructions* on page 80. Sew beads to necklaces on figures, using photo as your guide. Insert dowels through hems. Sew ends closed.

Handle—Make 2 each in MC, Color B, and Color C

With US 8 double-pointed needles, cast on 4 sts. Work knit cord as follows: * k4, without turning, slide sts to opposite end of needle, repeat from * until cord measures 55". Bind off. Fold and pin cords together to prevent tangling during felting. Felt cords, following *Felting Instructions* on page 80. After cords are felted, braid 3 cords—one of each color—for each handle, leaving 2½" unbraided at each end. Wrap MC tightly around end where braided part meets unbraided part to prevent braid from coming undone. Sew handles to bag 3½" from top (see photo). Sew snap to inside of bag at top centers.

Yei Figures - Front & Back Chart

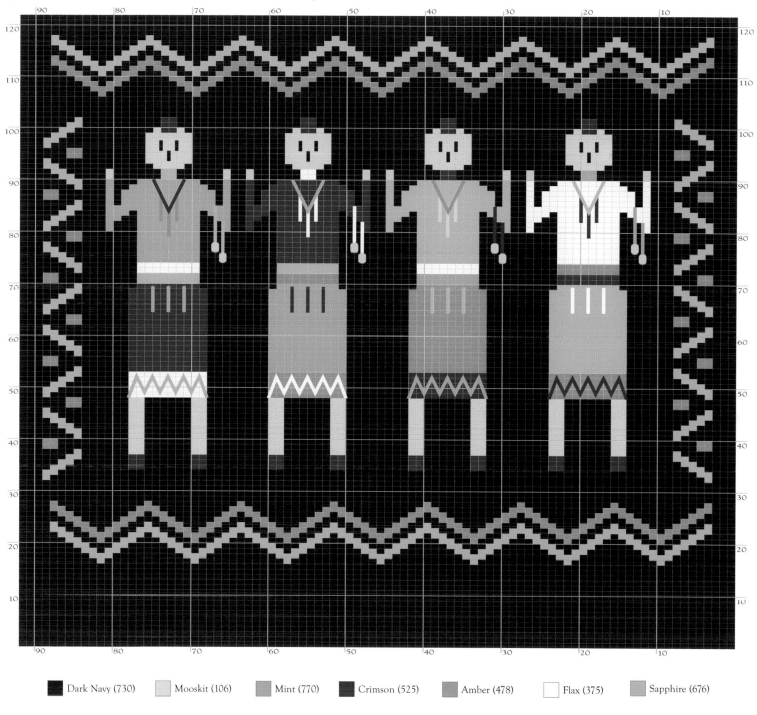

Dark Navy (730) Mooskit (106) Mint (770) Crimson (525) Amber (478) Flax (375) Sapphire (676)

Queen's Ball

Materials
Jamieson's Shetland Heather Aran—
300 grams Color A, Pippin (808)
250 grams Color B, Charcoal (126)

2 leather or vinyl soft black handles (approx. 18")
Polyfil™ (small amounts to fill balls)
Small stitch holders
Tapestry needle

Needles
US 11 (8 mm), *or size needed to obtain gauge*
Set of double-pointed US 9 (5.5 mm)

Size
Approx. 20" wide x 22" high *before felting*
Approx. 17" wide x 15" high *after felting*

Gauge
13 sts/16 rows = 4" in stockinette stitch on US 11

Queen's Ball

Balls—Make 20

With US 11 and Color A, cast on 8 sts, leaving a long tail.

Row 1 (RS) Knit into front and back of every st—16 sts.

Rows 2, 4, 6, 8 & 10 Purl.

Rows 3, 5, 7 & 9 Knit.

Row 11 * K2tog, rep from *—8 sts.

Row 12 * P2tog, rep from *—4 sts.

Row 13 K2tog, k2—3 sts.

Change to US 9 double-pointed needle. Work knit cord as follows: * k3, without turning, slide sts to opposite end of needle, repeat from * until cord measures 3½". Place sts on holder. Thread cast-on tail onto tapestry needle, run through cast-on sts, pull tightly and secure. Stuff ball loosely with Polyfil™, leave on holder and sew side seam.

Front

With US 11 and Color B, cast on 65 sts. Work in stockinette stitch for 5", ending with RS facing for next row.

Next Row (RS) Knit.

Next Row Knit.

Work Rows 1-44 (below) twice.

Rows 1, 3, 5, 7, 9, 13, 15, 17, 19 & 21 (RS) K13A, k13B, k13A, k13B, k13A.

Rows 2, 4, 6, 8, 10, 12, 14, 16, 18, 20 & 22 P13A, p13B, p13A, p13B, p13A.

Row 11 * K5A, *Attach Ball**, k5A, k13B, repeat from * once, k5A, *Attach Ball**, k5A.

Rows 23, 25, 27, 29, 31, 35, 37, 39, 41 & 43 K13B, k13A, k13B, k13A, k13B.

Rows 24, 26, 28, 30, 32, 34, 36, 38, 40, 42 & 44 P13B, p13A, p13B, p13A, p13B.

Row 33 * K13B, k5A, *Attach Ball**, k5A, repeat from * once, k13B.

Attach Ball - With RS facing, slide 3 cord sts from holder onto double-pointed needle, hold in front of needle with bag sts, and with third US 11, knit 3 cord sts together with 3 bag sts.

Change to garter stitch and [work 4 rows of Color B, 4 rows of Color A] 4 times. Bind off.

Back

Work same as for front.

Side Panels—Make 2

With US 11 and Color B, cast on 13 sts.

Next Row (RS) Knit.

New Row Knit.

Work Rows 1-44 (below) twice.

Rows 1, 3, 5, 7, 9, 11, 13, 15, 17, 19 & 21 (RS) K13B.

Rows 2, 4, 6, 8, 10, 12, 14, 16, 18, 20 & 22 P13B.

Rows 23, 25, 27, 29, 31, 35, 37, 39, 41 & 43 K13A.

Rows 24, 26, 28, 30, 32, 34, 36, 38, 40, 42 & 44 P13A.

Row 33 K5A, *Attach Ball**, k5A.

Change to Color B and continue in stockinette stitch for 1½". Bind off.

Pocket

With US 11 and Color B, cast on 32 sts. Work in stockinette stitch for 10". Bind off.

Felting & Finishing

Center pocket on inside back of bag approx. 3" from top and sew down. Overlap bottoms of bag and sew bottom seams. Insert side panels and sew seams. Fold hem and sew to inside. Felt bag, following *Felting Instructions* on page 80. Sew handles to outside of bag approx. 1" from top.

Jacobean

Materials
Jamieson's Shetland Double Knitting—
200 grams MC, Grouse (235)
50 grams Moss (147)
50 grams Granny Smith (1140)
50 grams Chartreuse (365)
50 grams Chestnut (577)
50 grams Cinnamon (576)
25 grams Coral (540)
25 grams Burnt Umber (1190)

Two ½" dowels—approx. 15" long
6½ x 16" piece of buckram stiffener for bag bottom
Tapestry needle

Needles
US 7 (4.5 mm), *or size needed to obtain gauge*
Set of double-pointed US 4 (3.5 mm)

Size
Approx. 17" wide x 9" high *before felting*
Approx. 15" wide x 7½" high *after felting*

Gauge
20 sts/27 rows = 4" in stockinette stitch on US 7

Jacobean

Notes

Knit back, front and bottom of bag in one piece, beginning at back hem and working downwards towards bottom of bag, then working upwards to front hem. Work **Chart** in stockinette stitch using intarsia method. Work embroidered details afterwards.

Back Hem—Dowel Casing

With US 7 and MC, cast on 90 sts. Beginning with a RS (knit) row, work 4 rows in stockinette stitch.

Turning Ridge

Next Row (RS) Knit.
Next Row Knit.
Next Row Knit.

Back

Beginning with a purl row, work 3 rows in stockinette stitch. Continuing in stockinette stitch, work the 58 rows of **Chart** using intarsia method. *Odd-numbered rows are RS rows and even-numbered rows are WS rows.* Change to MC and work base as follows:

Turning Ridge

Next Row (RS) Knit.
Next Row Knit.
Next Row Knit.

Bottom

Beg with WS (purl) row, continue in stockinette stitch until base measures 7½" from turning ridge, ending with RS facing for next row.

Turning Ridge

Next Row (RS) Knit.
Next Row Knit.
Next Row Knit.

Front

Continuing in stockinette stitch, work the 58 rows of **Chart** *IN REVERSE ORDER. Odd-numbered rows are RS rows and even-numbered rows are WS rows.* Beginning with a WS row, work 3 rows in stockinette stitch, then work front hem as follows:

Turning Ridge

Next Row (RS) Knit.
Next Row Knit.
Next Row Knit.

Front Hem—Dowel Casing

Continue in stockinette stitch for 4 rows. Bind off. Fold hems and sew to inside, leaving ends open to insert dowels later.

Side Panels

With US 7 and MC, RS facing, pick up 41 sts along short end of base. Work in stockinette stitch until piece measures same length as back and front (about 9"), ending with WS facing for next row.

Next Row (WS) Knit.
Next Row Knit.

Continue in stockinette stitch for another 1¼" for facing. Bind off. Repeat for opposite side panel.

Bottom Facing

With US 7 and MC, cast on 89 sts. Work in stockinette stitch until piece measures 7½". Bind off.

Handles

With double-pointed US 4 and MC, cast on 5 sts. * k5, without turning, slide sts to opposite end of needle, repeat from * until cord measures 84". Bind off. Fold cord in half, anchor at center and twist each half until cord kinks. Fold in half again and let the ends twist back on each other. Secure ends so cords don't untwist.

Felting & Finishing

Sew bottom facing, leaving one short end open to insert stiffener later. Fold side panel hems and sew to inside. Sew side panels to back and front, leaving one end open (you'll close this end after dowels are inserted—after felting). Make pleats in sides as shown in photograph. Stitch through all layers to secure. Insert ends of handles between pleats and sew in place. Felt bag, following **Felting Instructions** on page 80. Insert dowels into top hems. Sew ends closed. Cut buckram to fit inside bottom. Insert into bottom and sew end closed.

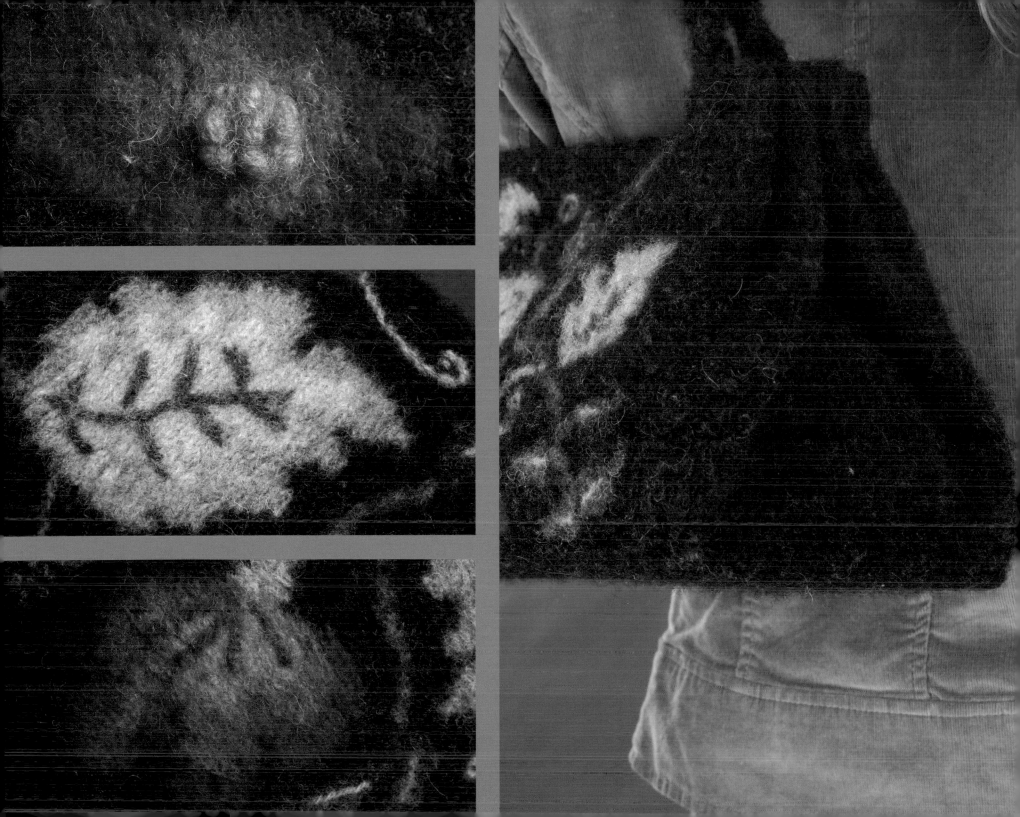

Jacobean

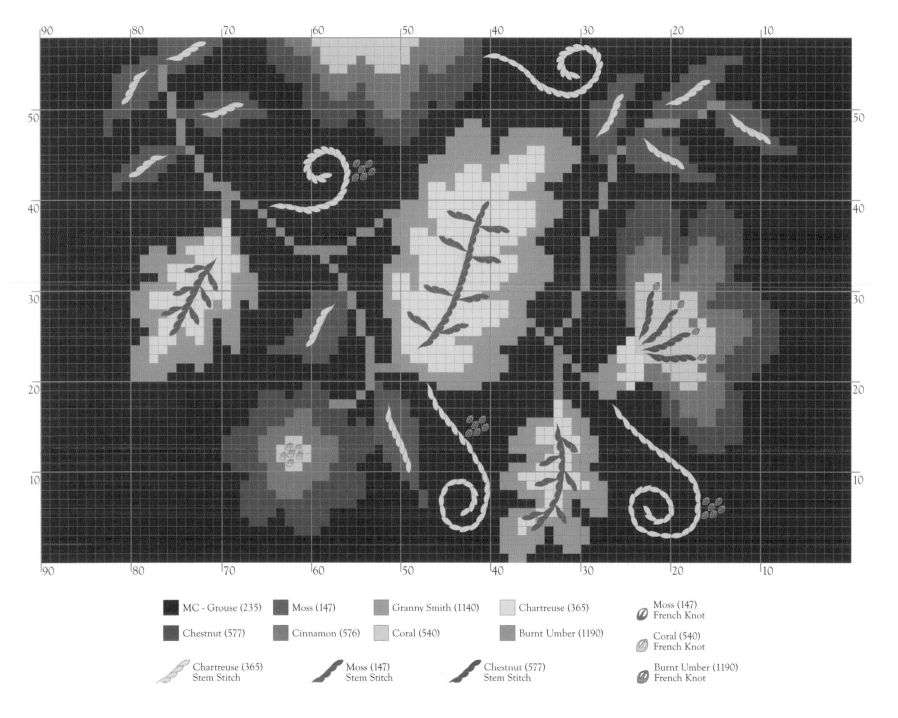

	MC - Grouse (235)		Moss (147)		Granny Smith (1140)		Chartreuse (365)		Moss (147) French Knot
	Chestnut (577)		Cinnamon (576)		Coral (540)		Burnt Umber (1190)		Coral (540) French Knot
	Chartreuse (365) Stem Stitch		Moss (147) Stem Stitch		Chestnut (577) Stem Stitch				Burnt Umber (1190) French Knot

Wisteria

Materials
Jamieson's Shetland Heather Aran—
200 grams Color A, Nightshade (1401)
50 grams Color B, Conifer (336)
50 grams Color C, Horizon (164)
50 grams Color D, Amethyst (1310)

Jamieson's Shetland Double Knitting—
25 grams Color E, Anemone (616)
50 grams Color F, Pistachio (791)
50 grams Color G, Moss (147)

120 small, round beads
Tapestry needle

Needles
US 9 (5.5 mm), *or size needed to obtain gauge*
Set of double-pointed US 8 (5 mm)

Size
Approx. 16" wide x 20" high *before felting*
Approx. 14" wide x 17" high *after felting*

Gauge
14 sts/22 rows = 4" in stockinette stitch on US 9

Wisteria

Front

With US 9 and Color A, cast on 40 sts. Knit 1 row. Continue in stockinette stitch, **AND AT SAME TIME**, cast on 2 sts at beginning of next 6 rows, then increase 1 st at beginning of next 8 rows—60 sts. Continue without further shaping until piece measures 16" from cast-on edge, ending with RS facing for next row.

Shape Top

Next Row (RS) Bind off 8 sts, k12, attach new yarn, bind off next 16 sts, knit to end.
Next Row Bind off 8 sts, purl to end.

Working each side separately, continue as follows:

Next Row Ssk, knit to last 2 sts, k2tog.
Next Row Purl.

Rep last 2 rows until 4 sts remain. Place sts on holder.

Back

Work same as for front.

Side and Bottom Insert

With US 9 and Color A, cast on 18 sts. Work in stockinette stitch until piece measures 48" or correct length to fit around sides and bottom of bag. Bind off. Sew this piece to back and front to form bag body.

Make Cords & Handles

With US 8 double-pointed needles and Color B, cast on 5 sts. * K5, do not turn work, slide sts to opposite end of needle, repeat from *. Bind off. Make two 14" long cords for front and back tops of bag, two 18" long for side tops of bag, and four 19" long cords for handles. Sew 14" cords along top of front and back of bag. Sew 18" cords along top of each side of bag.

Finish Top of Bag

With US 9 and Color B, WS facing, beginning at one of the top corners, pick up 3 sts along end of cord, knit 4 sts from holder, pick up 3 sts along end of adjacent—10 sts. Knit 4 rows. Bind off. Repeat for remaining 3 corners.

Handles

* Twist 2 of the 19" cord lengths together and sew each end to inside tops of one side, rep from * for other side.

Flowers—Make 10 Each of Colors C, D & E

Make slip knot. * With US 9, cast on 4 sts, bind off 4 sts. Slip remaining st to left-hand needle, repeat from * until there are 7 petals. Tie off last st. Thread cast on tail onto tapestry needle, run through top loops of slip st, pull tightly to form flower. Tie cast-on and bound-off tails together.

Leaves—Make 26

With US 9 and Color G, cast on 5 sts.

Row 1 (RS) K2, yo, k1, yo, k2—7 sts.
Row 2 (and all WS rows) Purl.
Row 3 K3, yo, k1, yo, k3—9 sts.
Row 5 K4, yo, k1, yo, k4—11 sts.
Row 7 Ssk, k7, k2tog—9 sts.
Row 9 Ssk, k5, k2tog—7 sts.
Row 11 Ssk, k3, k2tog—5 sts.
Row 13 Ssk, k1, k2tog—3 sts.
Row 15 Slip 1, k2tog, psso—1 st. Fasten off.

Leaf Centers—Make 26

With US 9 and Color F, cast on 5 sts.

Row 1 (RS) K2, yo, k1, yo, k2—7 sts.
Row 2 (and all WS rows) Purl.
Row 3 K3, yo, k1, yo, k3—9 sts.
Row 5 Ssk, k5, k2tog—7 sts.
Row 7 Ssk, k3, k2tog—5 sts.
Row 9 Ssk, k1, k2tog—3 sts.
Row 11 Slip 1, k2tog, psso–1 st. Fasten off.

Felting & Finishing

Sew leaf centers on top of leaves. Sew leaves and flowers to bag as shown in photograph. Felt bag, following **Felting Instructions** on page 80. Sew beads to flower centers.

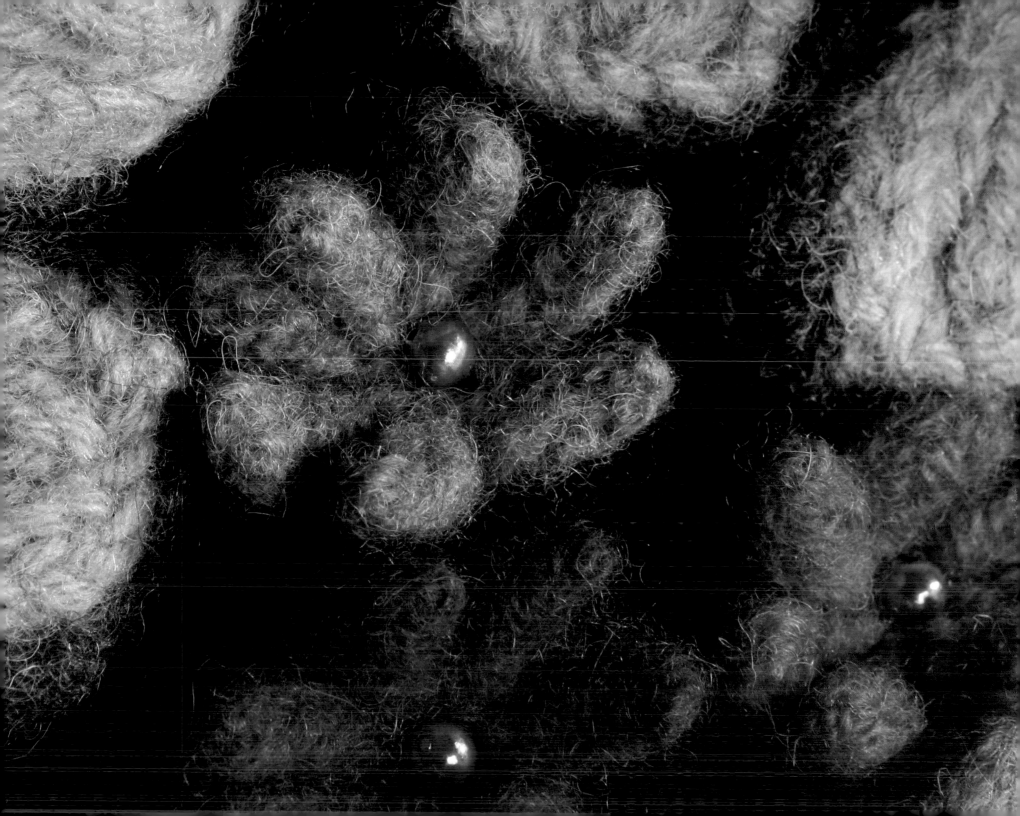

Purple Roses

Materials
Jamieson's Shetland Double Knitting—
150 grams Color A, Hyacinth (615)
50 grams Color B, Anemone (616)

4½" silver purse frame with loops
  (LV60 from Lacis—www.lacis.com)
Approx. 26" of bead fringe
Tapestry needle

Needles
US 9 (5.5 mm), *or size needed to obtain gauge*

Size
Approx. 12" wide at bottom/8" wide at top x 12" high
  before felting
Approx. 9" wide at bottom/6" wide at top x 8" high
  after felting

Gauge
18 sts/22 rows = 4" in stockinette stitch on US 9

Front

With US 9 and Color A, cast on 51 sts. Work in stockinette stitch for 16 rows, ending with RS facing for next row. Continue in stockinette stitch, **AND AT SAME TIME**, decrease 1 st at beginning and end of next row, then every 10th row thereafter 4 more times—41 sts. Continue in stockinette stitch until piece measures 12" from CO edge, ending with RS facing for next row.

Make Hem
Next Row (RS) Purl.

Continue in stockinette stitch for ¾". Bind off.

Back
Work same as for front.

Join Front & Back
Sew bottom seam. Sew side seams from bottom, leaving 3½" up to hem unsewn at top. Fold hem and sew to inside.

Roses—Make 16 each of Colors A and B
With US 9, cast on 10 sts.

Row 1 (RS) Knit.
Row 2, 4, 6 & 8 Purl.
Row 3 * Knit into front and back of st, repeat from *—20 sts.
Row 5 * Knit into front and back of st, repeat from *—40 sts.
Row 7 * Knit into front and back of st, repeat from *—80 sts.
Row 9 Bind off in knit.

Roll up on cast-on edge to form rose. Sew into place.

Cord
With US 9 and Color A, cast on 75 sts. Bind off.

Felting & Finishing
Felt roses, bag and cord, following **Felting Instructions** on page 80. Sew roses to bag, alternating colors as shown in photograph. Sew bead fringe around bottom of bag. Sew bag to frame and attach cord through frame loops.

Abbondanza

Materials
Jamieson's Shetland Heather Aran—
550 grams MC, Cedar (1060)
50 grams Color A, Oceanic (692)
50 grams Color B, Conifer (336)
50 grams Color C, Pippin (808)
50 grams Color D, Burnt Umber (1190)
50 grams Color E, Gingersnap (331)
50 grams Color F, Husk (383)
50 grams Color G, Lacquer (1220)
50 grams Color H, Amethyst (1310)

5" x 18" piece of heavy cardboard
2 silver purse hooks
  (#HLN from Sunbelt—www.sunbeltfasteners.com)
One 1" leather button
Tapestry needle

Needles
US 11 (8 mm), *or size needed to obtain gauge*
Set of double-pointed US 9 (5.5 mm)

Size
20" wide x 21" high *before felting*
18" wide x 14" high *after felting*

Gauge
17 sts/24 rows = 4" in stockinette stitch on US 11

Front

With US 11 and MC, cast on 81 sts. Work in stockinette stitch until piece measures 6" from cast-on edge, ending with RS facing for next row.

Make Turning Ridge

Next Row (RS) Purl.

Next Row Purl.

Continue in stockinette stitch for another 19½". Work in garter st for 1". Bind off.

Back

Work same as for front up to garter stitch. Mark each side. Continue in stockinette stitch for 5½". Bind off 3 sts at beginning of next 12 rows—45 sts. Bind off.

Front Flap Edging

With US 11, RS facing, pick up 128 sts along top edge of flap.

Next Row (WS) Knit.

Next Row Knit.

With WS facing, bind off.

Side Panels

With US 11 and MC, pick up 28 sts along short edge of bottom of bag. Work in stockinette stitch for 19½", then work in garter stitch for 1". Bind off. Repeat for opposite side.

Berries—Make 17 with Color G and 15 with Color H

With US 11, cast on 1 st.

Row 1 (RS) Knit into front and back of stitch until there are 5 sts on needle.

Row 2 Purl.

Row 3 Knit.

Row 4 Purl.

Row 5 Ssk, k1, k2tog—1 st.

Row 6 Slip 1, p2tog, psso. Fasten off.

2-Color Leaves

Make 4 leaves with Colors F & E, 9 with Colors D & B; 3 with Colors C & A, and 1 with Colors B and E. Work the following instructions for each 2-color leaf, replacing MC with the first color given, and CC with the second color given.

With US 11 and MC, cast on 5 sts.

Row 1 (RS) With MC, K2, yo, k1, yo, k2—7 sts.

Row 2 With MC, purl.

Row 3 With MC, k3, yo, k1, yo, join CC and k3—9 sts.

Row 4 With CC, p4, with MC, p5.

Row 5 With MC, k4, yo, k1, yo, with CC, k4—11 sts.

Row 6 With CC, p5, with MC, p6.

Row 7 With MC, bind off 3 sts, [k1, yo] twice, with CC, k5—10 sts.

Row 8 With CC, bind off 3 sts, p1, with MC, p5—7 sts.

Row 9 With MC, k3 [yo, k1] twice, with CC, k2—9 sts.

Row 10 With CC, p3, with MC, p6.

Row 11 With MC, k4, [yo, k1] twice, with CC, k3—11 sts.

Row 12 With CC, p4, with MC, p7.

Row 13 With MC, bind off 3 sts, [k1, yo] twice, k1, with CC, k4—10 sts.

Row 14 With CC, bind off 3 sts, p1, with MC, p5—7 sts.

Row 15 With MC, ssk, k2, with CC, k1, k2tog—5 sts.

Row 16 With CC, p3, with MC, p2.

Row 17 With MC, ssk, with CC, k1, k2tog—3 sts.

Row 18 With CC, p3.

Row 19 With CC, slip 1, k2tog, psso—1 st. Fasten off.

Make 3 leaves in 3-color combinations of your choice. Work as above, introducing the 3rd color in the last few rows.

Abbondanza

Cord

With US 9 double-pointed needles and Color C, cast on 3 sts. * K3, without turning, slide sts to opposite end of needle, repeat from * until cord measures approx. 29". Bind off. Make 3 more cords, each approx. 16".

Aspen Leaf—Make 20

With US 11 and Color B, cast on 5 sts.

Row 1 (RS) K2, yo, k1, yo, k2—7 sts.
Row 2 (and all WS rows) Purl.
Row 3 K3, yo, k1, yo, k3—9 sts.
Row 5 K4, yo, k1, yo, k4—11 sts.
Row 7 Ssk, k7, k2tog—9 sts.
Row 9 Ssk, k5, k2tog—7 sts.
Row 11 Ssk, k3, k2tog—5 sts.
Row 13 Ssk, k1, k2tog—3 sts.
Row 15 Slip 1, k2tog, psso—1 st. Fasten off.

Palm Leaf—Make 6 with Color C and 6 with Color A

With US 11, cast on 3 sts. Work in stockinette stitch, increasing 1 st at beginning and end of every RS row 3 times—9 sts. Work without further shaping for 8 rows, ending with RS facing for next row. Decrease as follows:

Row 1 (RS) Ssk, knit to last 2 sts, k2tog—2 sts decreased.
Row 2 Purl.

Rep Rows 1-2 above until 3 sts remain.

Next Row (RS) Slip 1, k2tog, psso–1 st. Fasten off.

Handle—Make 2

With US 11 and MC, cast on 15 sts. Work in stockinette stitch until handle measures 38". Bind off.

Felting & Finishing

Sew cords and leaves to front and back using photographs and schematic below a general guide. Attach berries by pulling cast-on tail and bind-off tail through front and tying to back. Thread cast-on and bind-off tail and bring through berry to front; cut tails (this gets rid of tails). With Color D, work embroidery on palm leaf. Sew side panels to front, then back, overlap bottom panels, sew one to inside along turning ridge and one to outside along turning ridge. Sew one side of overlap closed, leaving other side open. Felt bag, following **Felting Instructions** on page 80. After piece is felted, cut cardboard to fit bottom. Slide through bottom opening and sew seam. Sew overlap leaves from front and back to sides. Sew button to center front. Sew handle hooks to each end of knit handle. Sew end of handles to each side of bag on first fold of side panel insert.

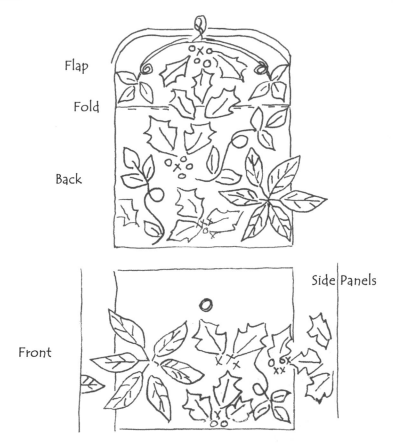

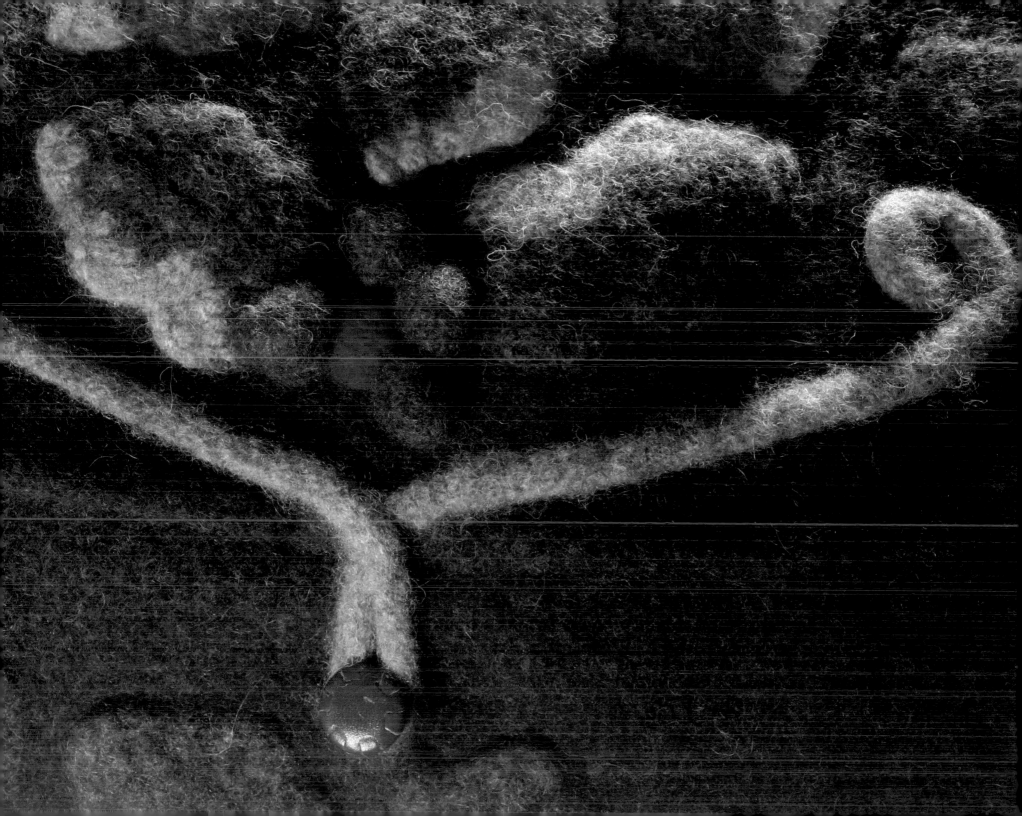

Frog

Materials
Jamieson's Shetland Heather Aran—
100 grams Color A, Conifer (336)
50 grams Color B, Pippin (808)
Small amount Color C, Lacquer (1220)
Small amount Color D, Husk (383)

Small amount of Polyfil™
Tapestry needle

Needles
US 11 (8 mm), *or size needed to obtain gauge*

Size
Approx. 11½" wide x 12½" high *before felting with
 flap folded*
Approx. 8½" wide x 9" high *after felting*

Gauge
17 sts/24 rows = 4" in stockinette stitch on US 11

Frog

Back

With US 11 and Color A, cast on 25 sts. Work in stockinette stitch for 2 rows, then increase 1 st at beginning of every row until there are 35 sts on needle. Continue without further shaping until piece measures 11" from cast-on edge. Mark each side.

Flap

Continue in stockinette stitch for 5" more. Bind off 4 sts at beginning of next 6 rows. Bind off remaining 11 sts.

Mouth

With US 11 and Color C, RS facing, pick up 4 sts along side of flap, 41 sts across front of flap, and 4 sts along opposite side of flap. Knit 2 rows. Bind off in knit.

Front

With US 11 and Color B, work same as for back until piece measures 10½". Work in garter stitch for ½". Bind off.

Handle and Side Inserts

With US 11 and Color A, cast on 15 sts. Work in stockinette stitch for 60". Bind off. Sew cast-on edge to bound-off edge. Beginning at bottom center of back, pin and sew one side of insert around bag to markers. Sew other side of insert in place to bag front.

Tongue

With US 11 and Color C, cast on 14 sts. Work in stockinette stitch for 1½". Decrease 1 st at beginning and end of next row, then every 4th row until 2 sts remain. Knit 2 rows. Pass 1st st over 2nd st and fasten off. Sew to center bottom of flap, just under mouth.

Eyes

With US 11 and Color A, cast on 10 sts, leaving a long tail for seaming. Work as follows:

Row 1 (RS) * Knit into front and back of every st—20 sts.
Row 2 (and all WS rows) Purl.
Rows 3, 5, 7 & 9 Knit.
Row 11 Change to Color D and knit.
Row 13 * K2tog, repeat from * to end—10 sts.
Row 14 * P2tog, repeat from * end—5 sts remain. Pass 2nd, 3rd, 4th and 5th st over 1st st. Fasten off.

With tapestry needle, run thread through cast-on sts, gather and secure thread. Stuff lightly with Polyfil™. Sew side edges together.

Finishing

Eyes may need additional felting because of the Polyfil™. Hand agitate in hot/cold water a few times. Sew eyes to each top side of flap. Felt bag, following **Felting Instructions** on page 80. Tongue will flip up naturally.

Felting Instructions

Wash bag in machine on hot/cold cycle with an old pair of jeans and ¼ cup of liquid detergent. The jeans will help balance the load and aid in the felting process. Repeat wash cycle until desired felted texture and size are achieved. Shape the bag and let dry. Follow additional bag instructions when noted. Beads, feathers and hardware such as handles, dowels, buttons and straps should be added after felting. Make all pieces for each bag and felt at the same time to insure consistent felting. When felting a long cord length, fold and pin the length together using large safety pins or fold and fasten loosely with a rubber band or cotton or acrylic yarn. You can also put the cord into a small laundry bag to keep the cord from tangling around other pieces in the machine.

Facing page–Bobbles & Brambles shown in opposite colorway–before felting.

Acknowledgements

With knitting being so popular again, it's been a very busy year for me, so I am extra-grateful to my steadfast knitters, friends and co-workers who helped me complete this book. Many thanks to Eileen Curry, Dana Matuskey, Martina Browning, Meggan Walz, Mara Lloyd, Leslie Solomon, and Holly Neiding—the best knitters ever. My gratitude to David Codling and Gregory Courtney (tough taskmasters but great friends) for their support, inspiration, technical editing and beautiful graphic design. Thanks to Jan Stahl for her generosity in sharing her marvelous knitting staff with me and to Nancy Henderson, Rita Greenfeder and Heris Stenzel for their invaluable help. Thanks to my husband, Howard, who has helped me get through the completion of 10 books, to date, without the aid of tranquilizers. And last but not least . . . thank you to the "gods of the washing machine" who smiled favorably on my felting efforts.

Abbreviations

CC—contrasting color

k—knit

k2tog—knit 2 stitches together

MC—main color

m1 (make 1 st)—with point of right-hand needle, lift running thread between st just worked and next st, place on left-hand needle, and knit through back of loop.

p—purl

psso—pass the slipped stitch over the st just knitted

p2tog—purl 2 stitches together

RS—right side

ssk (slip, slip, knit)—slip 1 st as if to knit; slip another st as if to knit; slip both sts back to left-hand needle and knit them together through back loop.

st(s)—stitch(es)

wyib—with yarn in back

wyif—with yarn in front

WS—wrong side

yo (inc)—yarn over needle

Nicky Epstein is one of today's most prolific and versatile knitwear designers, authors and teachers. She has gained worldwide recognition for her artistic, distinctive and innovative work, whimsical sense of style and informative workshops. Her designs continue to be featured in many knitting magazines and publications, on television, and in museums. Nicky was recently honored by the National Needle Arts Association for her contributions to the knitting industry. *Knits For Barbie Doll* won the National Independent Book Publisher's Award as the Year's Best Craft Book. Other best-selling books include *The Knit Hat Book*, *Knitted Embellishments*, *Knitting For Your Home*, *Crochet For Barbie Doll*, and *Barbie And Me*. Her knitting resource books contain many of her original techniques and are considered "must-have" books for every knitter's library. *Knitting On The Edge* and *Knitting Over The Edge* have won critical acclaim and are fast becoming knitting classics. *Nicky Epstein's Knitted Flowers* and *Knitting Beyond The Edge* will be released in Fall 2006. Nicky lives in New York City and travels extensively in pursuit of creative inspiration.